Numbers, Shapes, & Sizes

Written by
Roberta Schomburg, Ph.D.
Hedda Bluestone Sharapan

Editorial Consultants:
Cathy Cohen Droz
Elaine Lynch
Aisha White

Editor:
Joellyn Thrall Cicciarelli

Illustrator:
Ben Mahan

Designer:
Moonhee Pak

Project Director:
Carolea Williams

CTP 1999 Creative Teaching Press, Inc., Huntington Beach, CA 92649
1999 Family Communications, Inc., Pittsburgh, PA 15213
Reproduction of activities in any manner for use in the classroom and not for commercial sale is permissible.
Reproduction of these materials for an entire school or for a school system is strictly prohibited.

Table of Contents

A Letter from Fred Rogers 3

Introduction 4

Helpful Suggestions for Using This Book 5

Numbers
Matching Pairs 6
Looking for Numbers 7
How Many Times? 8
Ball Bounce 9
Boxes inside Boxes 10
Sorting Buttons 11
Learn about Money 12

Shapes
Spinning Circles 13
Things That Are Round 14
Wheel Toys 15
Blocks 16
My Shape It Has Three Corners 17
Three-Cornered Hats 18
Vegetable Prints 19
Outline Match 20
Sorting Paper Shapes 21
Shape Designs 22
Connect-the-Dot Designs 23
Puzzles 24

Sizes & Measurements
Pouring Rice 25
Making a Graph 26
Comparing Sizes 27
How Long? 28
Comparing Weights 29
Measuring Time 30
Sand Clock 31

Mister Rogers' Neighborhood Television Program References . . 32

A Letter from Fred Rogers

Dear Neighbor,

As far as children and learning go, I've come to believe a very simple statement: Children can learn almost anything both easily and well so long as they are "ready" to learn. That does sound simple. What's not simple about it, of course, is just what it means for a child to be "ready."

How do we know when a child is "ready" to learn about such things as math concepts? Readiness comes from within, and you can hear it when a child shows interest in numbers, counting, and comparing . . . or when a child asks questions like *How many are there?*, or asks someone to *count with me*, or writes down a certain number—an age, a phone number, or an address.

Play is one of the most important things that can help a child be "ready" to learn about anything, even math. As children work with blocks and crayons, miniature figures and trucks, or even just a variety of odds and ends, they are constantly learning about how things go together in the world, how they can use symbols to express their ideas, and how they can communicate so others can understand. And, of course, aren't those all important foundations for the understanding of mathematical concepts?

As you help children appreciate their real-life experiences playing with things like numbers, shapes, and measurements, you will be helping them learn that math can have relevance in all people's lives. When children care about what they're learning and when they know their teachers care about them, they are more likely to be ready to learn and grow . . . and eventually "do math."

Fred Rogers

Introduction

Welcome to *Numbers, Shapes, & Sizes!* In this book you'll find lots of activities to help children learn about the way the world is organized by shape, size, space, and much more!

When children learn about concepts relating to numbers, shapes, and sizes, they begin to see and compare the similarities and differences between objects in their world. Conceptual thinking begins when children become interested in matching things, categorizing, and labeling objects. As children explore numbers, shapes, and sizes, they begin to understand the basic concepts of time, measurement, and quantity—concepts they will use every day for the rest of their lives.

The activities presented in this book can give you ways to help children understand the concepts of number, shape, and size as they grow and learn.

Here are some things to keep in mind when you're planning these activities:

- These activities have been designed to offer learning opportunities that appropriately match the ways young children think and incorporate information into their own everyday lives. Young children learn best through hands-on activities that give them ways to *experience, explore,* and *express* their thoughts and feelings.

- The activities in this book focus on *how* children learn rather than *what* they learn because the process of learning is more important than any particular content. For example, it's important that young children learn *how* to categorize and name objects, but it is far less important *what* the objects are (i.e., colors, cars, coins, or whatever interests the children).

- Give yourself freedom in planning. You can incorporate the activities into your regular math curriculum, or use them throughout the year as appropriate situations arise. For example, "Wheel Toys" on page 15 would be a great activity to offer on a day when the children use riding toys.

Learning about numbers, shapes, and sizes helps children develop important life skills. As you work on the activities in this book, the children will learn to understand the concept of number, solve problems in a logical way, and gain a sense of self-confidence as they learn about new ideas.

Helpful Suggestions for Using This Book

Consider the following suggestions for using this book as you plan how to present the activities to the children:

- This book is divided into three sections: *Numbers, Shapes,* and *Sizes & Measurements.* It's a good idea to read each section "opener" before trying an activity. Each section begins with a short paragraph that describes why the activities within the section are important. In addition, each opener offers a list of Literature Links—related picture books to bring into the class.

- Take a few minutes to review an activity before "diving in." Most of the activities are meant for small groups, but some may work fine with the entire class. Reviewing the activity beforehand can help you decide what would work best in your class.

  - Set boundaries. Children are more comfortable when adults let them know what the limits are. It's a good idea to let the children know in advance your rules about using materials. The activities are more meaningful if the children know what is expected of them.

    - Show interest in the children's ideas. You certainly don't have to understand all that a child may be communicating through his or her creative efforts. What's important is letting the children know you respect their attempts to express whatever is on their mind at the moment. When you show interest in their ideas, you're showing the children that you care about them.

  - Sometimes a child may not feel like participating. It can be hard to know why a child doesn't feel ready to join in, but there is usually a good reason. It's fine for a child to simply watch the activity or have some quiet private play nearby.

- Feel free to adapt the activities for children with special needs. By making some changes in environment or materials, you can make the activities accessible for a child who has a special challenge.

- A list of *Mister Rogers' Neighborhood* television program references and information about viewing and videotaping programs are provided on page 32. Consult this page to obtain information about viewing programs that correlate with activities in this book.

Numbers

Learning about numbers is much more than learning how to count to ten. Little by little, through lots of everyday experiences with objects, children come to understand what numbers represent. When you give them a chance to observe, sort, arrange, count, and graph objects that they encounter every day, you are helping them learn about the relationship between quantity and the symbols that are used to represent quantity. As children explore numbers, concepts, and quantity, they learn about same and different, more and less, bigger and smaller, and a variety of other important concepts. Through hands-on experiences, children learn that numbers are not just symbols to write or words to repeat in order—they learn that numbers represent real things and real ideas.

Literature Links

Animal Numbers by Bert Kitchen

Count Me In: 44 Songs and Rhymes about Numbers edited by Brian Hunt

Feast for Ten by Cathryn Falwell

I Spy Two Eyes: Numbers in Art designed by Lucy Micklethwait

My Signing Book of Numbers by Patricia Gillen

Spiders, Spiders Everywhere by Rozanne Lanczak Williams (Creative Teaching Press)

Matching Pairs

"Matching Pairs" can help children
- develop an awareness of similarities and differences.
- learn to look carefully.

Talk with the children about pairs of things. Explain that *pair* means two objects that go together, such as a pair of socks, a pair of shoes, or a pair of mittens. To demonstrate, show the children a pair of socks, and have them count the number.

Place pairs of similar objects in a large box, such as four pairs of socks with different patterns. One at a time, let each child pull an object from the box and try to find its match. After each child makes a match, ask him or her to count the objects he or she is holding. If you need to make this activity easier, place pairs of very different items in a box, such as a pair of shoes, a pair of mittens, a pair of socks, and a pair of slippers.

Materials
- several pairs of objects (shoes, gloves, mittens, socks, etc.)
- large box

Looking for Numbers

"Looking for Numbers" can help children
- recognize and use symbols.
- use numbers to communicate concepts.
- learn to recognize numbers.

In advance, make a blank book for each child by folding in half two pieces of construction paper and stapling them together along the fold.

To begin, write each child's name on the chalkboard. Ask each child to tell you how old he or she is and hold up his or her fingers to show the age. Beside each name, write that child's age. Explain that the numbers on the board represent how many years old each child is.

Show the children old calendar pages, and ask them to point out numbers they know. Give each child a blank book and a calendar page, and ask him or her to write *Numbers I Like* on the cover. Then have the children cut out six numbers from their calendar page and paste or glue each number to a different book page. (The outside back cover will remain blank.) Encourage each child to draw objects or use paste or glue to attach magazine pictures or old playing cards on each page to show the number of objects each number represents. Invite the children to "read" their finished book to the class.

☞ **Note to the Teacher:** *To encourage interest in numbers, have children practice counting objects with you, such as buttons on a shirt, blocks in a tower, children in the class, or chairs at a table.*

Materials
- construction paper
- stapler
- old calendar pages
- scissors
- crayons or markers
- paste or glue
- magazine pictures or old playing cards

How Many Times?

"How Many Times?" can help children
- recognize and use symbols.
- practice taking turns.

Show the children a game spinner, and have them say aloud together the numbers displayed on it. Then ask the children to help you prepare a game that uses those numbers. To begin, encourage each child to suggest an action such as

- *Clap your hands.*
- *Whisper "No, thank you."*
- *Turn around.*
- *Touch your toes.*
- *Shout "Yes, please."*
- *Say your name.*
- *Knock on the door or floor.*

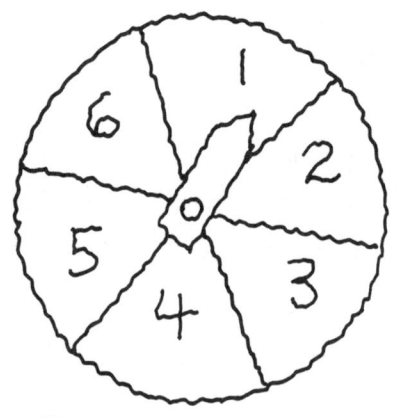

Write each child's suggestion on an index card. Mix up the cards, and place them face-down next to the game spinner. One at a time, let each child choose a card. After each card is drawn, have a child spin the spinner to see how many times he or she has to do what the card says. For example, if the spinner stops on the number four and the card says *Say your name*, the child says his or her name four times. Play the game until each child has a turn.

Materials
- game spinner with numbers
- index cards

Numbers

Ball Bounce

"Ball Bounce" can help children
- develop coordination.
- use numbers to communicate concepts.
- develop the ability to keep on trying.

Write each number from one to nine on a separate index card. Show each number card to the children, and encourage them to tell you the name of each number. Tell the children that each number represents how many times they will do something with a ball.

If the weather permits, take the children outside, and give each child a rubber ball. Shuffle the cards, and ask a child to choose one. Have the child read the number aloud, and give the rest of the class a command that uses the number and the balls, such as
- *Bounce and catch the ball slowly three times.*
- *Touch the ball three times.*
- *Bounce the ball quickly three times.*
- *Hold the ball on your head and walk three steps.*

Play the game until each child has a chance to choose a number.

☞ **Note to the Teacher:** When the game is over, you could take the children inside, put on some music, and encourage them to pretend to bounce like balls—bouncing high, low, quickly, or slowly.

Materials
- index cards
- rubber ball for each child

Boxes inside Boxes

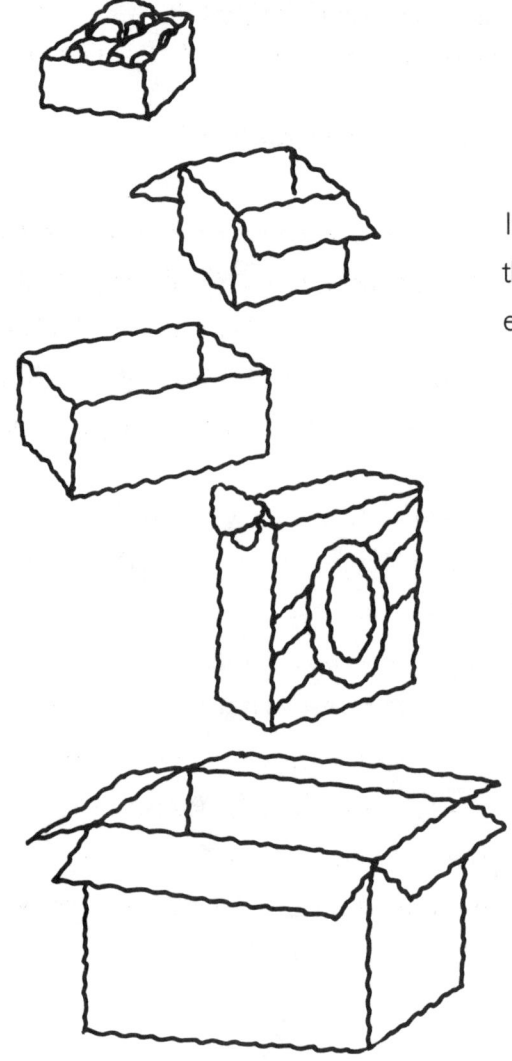

"Boxes inside Boxes" can help children
- learn to count objects.
- develop the ability to play creatively.
- practice taking turns.

In advance, without the children knowing, place a small toy in the smallest box of five boxes of graduated sizes. Then place each box inside the other.

To begin, place the set of boxes on the floor. Invite a child to open the biggest box and take out what's inside. Before the box is opened, have the class count. For example, the class could say *one box*. When the child takes the second box out of the first one, have the class say *two boxes*.

Continue having the children open the boxes and count until they get to the surprise inside.

After the counting game, encourage the children to use the boxes in whatever way they wish. For example, the children could
- put the boxes back together with a different surprise in the smallest box.
- build with them.
- use them for houses in their play.

☞ **Note to the Teacher:** *Children might enjoy playing with other sorts of nesting toys, such as Matrushka dolls.*

Materials
- small toy
- five boxes of graduated sizes (small ring box, necklace box, cereal box, gift box, shirt box, dress box, cardboard carton, etc.)

Sorting Buttons

"Sorting Buttons" can help children
- sort and classify according to likenesses and differences.
- use numbers to communicate concepts.

Place a variety of buttons in a dishpan or shallow box. Ask the children to tell you how the buttons are different. Divide the class into small groups, and give each group several plastic containers, a muffin tin, or an egg carton. Then encourage the children to decide how to sort the buttons, such as by
- color.
- size.
- number of holes.

Once the buttons are sorted, ask the children to count the buttons in each category. Have the children compare two categories and tell which category has the most buttons and which has the least buttons. Then encourage the children to sort the buttons in other ways.

Materials
- variety of buttons (some same, some different)
- dishpan or shallow box
- several plastic containers, muffin tins, or egg cartons

Numbers

Learn about Money

"Learn about Money" can help children
- develop an awareness of similarities and differences.
- learn more about their world.
- learn about money.

Have each child use thin paper and a pencil to make rubbings of several coins. Glue the rubbings to tagboard, and cut them out. Cut paper into strips, and help the children use green crayons or markers to draw designs on them to make "dollar bills." To make a pretend checkbook, staple several strips of paper together. Have children draw lines on the paper and then add words or symbols such as *Date*, *To*, *$*, and *Name*.

Place the "money" in the dramatic play area, and invite the children to use it in their play.

☞ **Note to the Teacher:** You may want to explain what checks are and how they are used.

Materials
- thin paper
- pencils
- several coins
- glue
- tagboard
- scissors
- paper
- green crayons or markers
- stapler

Numbers

Shapes

When you help children become aware of shapes, you give them a way to understand about objects in the world and how objects take up space. As children begin to understand, recognize, and name shapes, they gain skills that help them as they learn to write and draw. You also help them appreciate the three-dimensional, geometric, and physical properties of objects. There are dozens of everyday ways to help children gather information about shapes, such as by inviting them to talk about, touch, turn, and make different-shaped objects. Even pointing out different shapes found in nature or the children's environment can help them understand shapes. And through this understanding, children learn other things, such as how to move their bodies through space, use symbols, build with blocks, and look at things from different perspectives.

Literature Links

Architecture: Shapes
by Michael J. Crosbie

Making Shapes (Science for Fun)
by Gary Gibson

Sea Shapes by Susie MacDonald

Shape Space by Cathryn Falwell

Shapes (Toby and His Dog)
by Kath Mellentin

So Many Circles, So Many Squares
by Tana Hoban

Spinning Circles

"Spinning Circles" can help children
- learn more about shapes.
- develop fine motor skills.

In advance, cut out a tagboard circle for each child. Talk about circles, and invite the children to point out classroom objects that are round. Give each child a circle, and help the children divide their circle into four sections by drawing a large X through the center. Encourage the children to use crayons or markers to decorate their circle. (You might want to suggest that the children color each section a different color.)

Show the children how to poke a pencil through their circle and spin it. As the children spin their pencil, they will see the colors blend. To close, talk about how the circles remain round even when they are moving.

☞ **Note to the Teacher:** Older children might be able to trace around a pattern and cut out their own circles.

Materials

- 6" (15 cm) diameter tagboard circles
- scissors
- pencils
- crayons or markers

Things That Are Round

"Things That Are Round" can help children
- develop an awareness of similarities and differences.
- learn more about shapes.
- learn to look carefully.

In advance, place in a box several round objects, such as
- rings.
- paper plates.
- margarine lids.
- clocks or other dials.
- pots and pans.
- balls and other round toys.
- cabinet pulls and doorknobs.
- baskets, flowerpots, or trays.

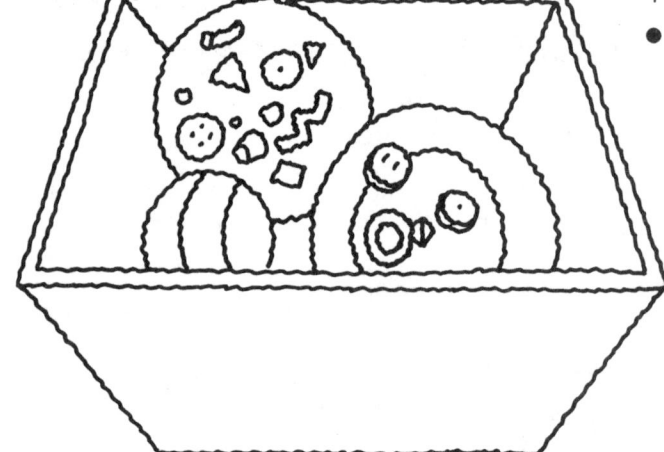

Ask the children to look around the room and name some things that are round. Then take each round item out of the box one at a time, and talk about the parts of it that are round. Encourage the children to touch each object and run their hands around the round parts.

Give each child a flat, round object, such as a margarine lid or pan top, and a piece of construction paper. Have children practice tracing circles on their paper. Then have the children decorate their circles with bits of round scrap material.

☞ **Note to the Teacher:** If the weather permits, take the class on a walk and have the children look for round things outside. The children might point out objects such as wheels, windows, or round signs.

Materials
- several round objects
- box
- construction paper
- crayons or markers
- round scrap material (buttons, paper circles, round stickers, etc.)
- paste or glue

Shapes

Wheel Toys

"Wheel Toys" can help children
- learn more about shapes.
- develop an awareness of similarities and differences.

Take the children outside, and have them point out all the wheels they can see, such as wheels on
- cars.
- buses.
- trucks.
- bicycles.

(If weather doesn't permit this, show the children pictures of different wheels.) Explain that wheels are round and that their shape allows them to roll.

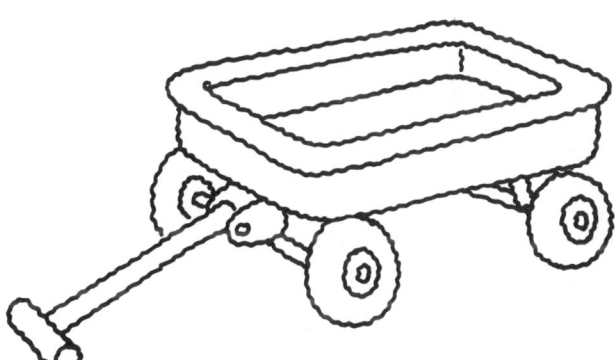

Back in class, let each child find a toy that has wheels to show to the class. Give the children plenty of time to play with the wheels of the toys. As the children play, ask
- *Can you make the wheels go fast?*
- *Can you make them go slow?*
- *What shape is a wheel?*

During recess, set out several toys with wheels, such as wagons, tricycles, and other riding toys, and invite the children to play with them.

Materials
- *books or magazines with pictures of wheels (optional)*
- *toys with wheels*
- *riding toys with wheels*

Blocks

"Blocks" can help children
- develop the ability to play creatively.
- learn more about their world.

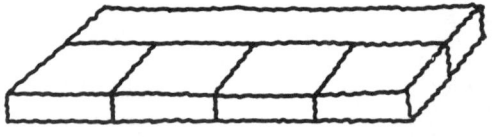

Let the children compare the sizes and shapes of wooden blocks. See how many ways the children can combine the blocks to make new shapes. For example, two triangles can make a square and four short blocks can equal the size of one long block.

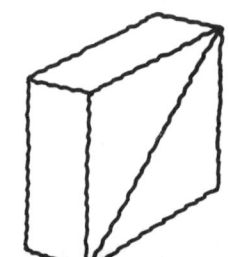

Then give each child a cardboard box or block of wood. Ask each child to cut out six animal pictures from an old magazine. Have the children tape each picture to a side of their box or block.

You can use the finished blocks in many ways. For example, you can
- turn one block at a time and ask the children to name each animal.
- have the children use the animal blocks with other small toys to set up and play with a pretend zoo, animal shelter, circus, or any other scene.
- hang the blocks from the ceiling for an interesting display.

Materials
- wooden blocks
- cardboard boxes or blocks of wood
- scissors
- old magazines with animal pictures
- tape

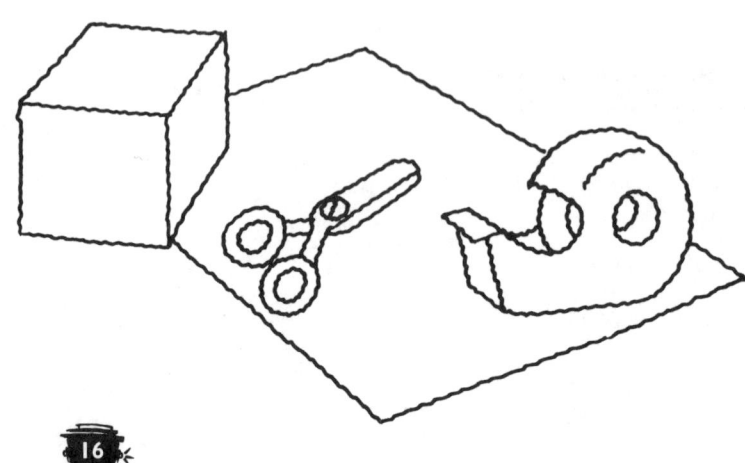

My Shape It Has Three Corners

"My Shape It Has Three Corners" can help children
- develop an awareness of similarities and differences.
- develop the ability to play creatively.

Give each child a piece of triangle-shaped fabric or a scarf folded into a triangle shape. Encourage the children to think of a way to use the fabric or scarf, such as
- wear it for dress-up play.
- use it as part of a dance.
- make a pretend bandage.
- wrap a baby doll in it.
- make a superhero cape.

Give the children plenty of time to play with the fabric pieces and scarves before collecting them.

☞ **Note to the Teacher:** You can store the fabric and scarves in your dramatic-play center so that children can continue to think of ways to use them in their dramatic play.

Materials
- fabric cut into triangle shapes or scarves folded into triangle shapes

Three-Cornered Hats

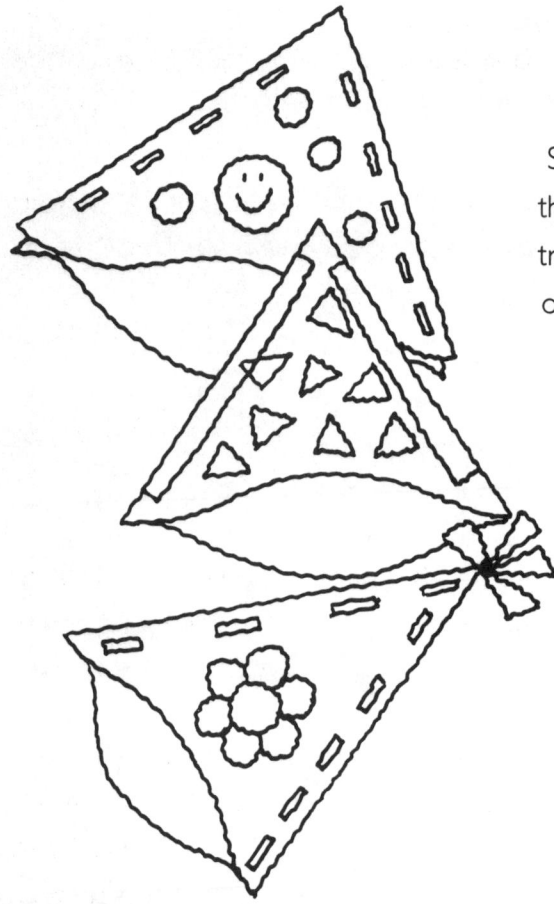

"Three-Cornered Hats" can help children
- develop the ability to play creatively.
- learn more about shapes.

Show the children a piece of triangle-shaped fabric. Tell them that the fabric has three sides and is cut into the shape of a triangle. Have the children look around the room for other objects that are shaped like triangles.

Then help the children make three-cornered hats. Give each child two large construction-paper triangles—one for the back of the hat and one for the front. Have the children make a hat large enough to fit their own head or make a smaller hat to fit a doll or stuffed animal. Staple or tape two sides of each hat together, leaving the bottom open. Be sure to space the bottom staples or tape carefully so the hat becomes the correct size for the child or a doll.

Have the children decorate their three-cornered hat with art supplies. To close, have a "triangle parade" during which each child marches while wearing a hat or holding a doll or a stuffed animal that wears a hat.

☞ **Note to the Teacher:** At snack time, you may want to serve the children sandwiches that have been cut into triangle shapes.

Materials

- *piece of triangle-shaped fabric*
- *large construction-paper triangles*
- *stapler or tape*
- *art supplies (crayons or markers, tissue paper, construction paper, streamers, pipe cleaners, stickers, buttons, paste or glue, ribbons, etc.)*
- *dolls or stuffed animals*

Vegetable Prints

"Vegetable Prints" can help children
- learn about shapes.
- learn more about foods.
- recognize and create patterns.

Show the children several vegetables, and ask the children if they know the name of each one. Talk about how the vegetables are alike and different in
- shape.
- color.
- size.

Cut the vegetables in half, or crosswise, in several pieces, so the children can see the inside part of the vegetables. Have the children tell you how the cut vegetables compare in shape, color, and size.

Demonstrate how to use the cut vegetables to make printed shapes on paper. Pour a little tempera paint into a shallow dish or tray. Show the children how to dip the cut end of a vegetable in the paint and use it to make prints on the paper.

Give each child a piece of construction paper, several vegetable pieces, and paint. Encourage the children to make their own designs or create patterns such as onion, onion, carrot, onion, onion, carrot.

When the prints are done, ask the children to tell you how the individual prints are alike and different from each other. Then encourage the children to match the real vegetables to their prints.

Materials
- vegetables (potato, onion, carrot, pepper, radish, etc.)
- knife
- cutting board
- tempera paint
- shallow dish or tray
- construction paper

Outline Match

"Outline Match" can help children
- learn to look carefully.
- develop an awareness of similarities and differences.
- learn more about shapes.
- develop fine motor skills.

Have the children help you trace a variety of different-shaped objects on a piece of butcher paper. As they trace, talk about each shape and name it.

After all the objects have been traced, mix them up, and invite each child to choose one. Have the children take turns matching the objects to their outlines on the paper.

☞ **Note to the Teacher:** For another game, use pots and pans with lids. See if the children can match the correct lid to each pot or pan. You might want to try the same game with plastic containers, plastic pitchers, or empty coffee cans with plastic lids.

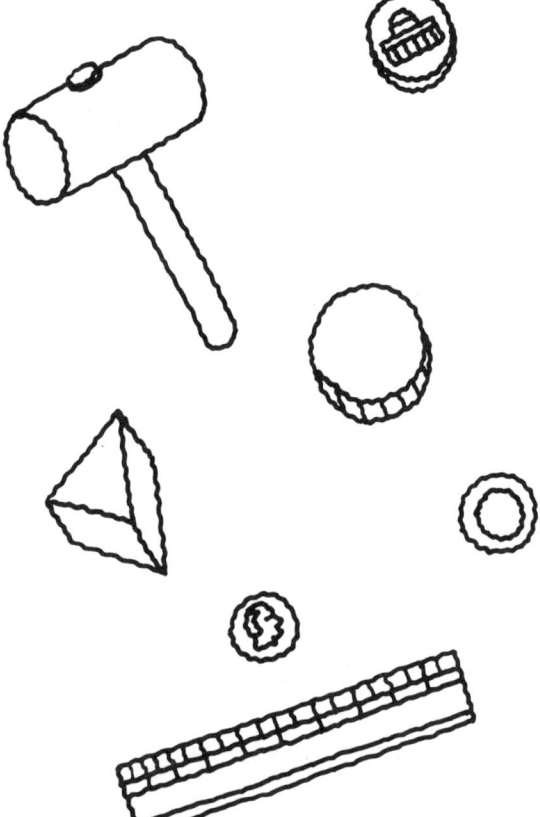

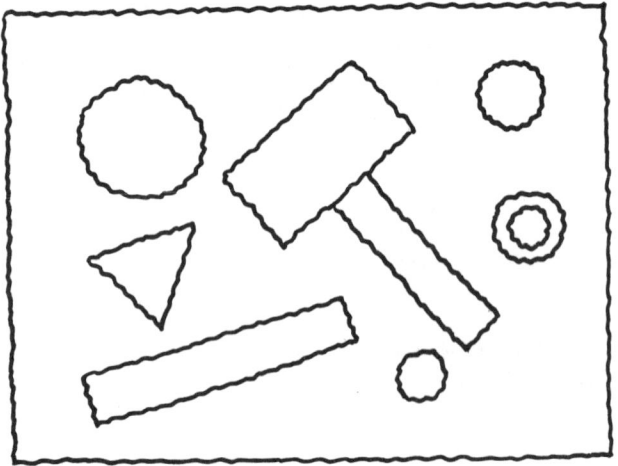

Materials
- butcher paper
- markers
- objects of different shapes (blocks, ruler, coin, envelope, margarine lid, etc.)

Shapes

Sorting Paper Shapes

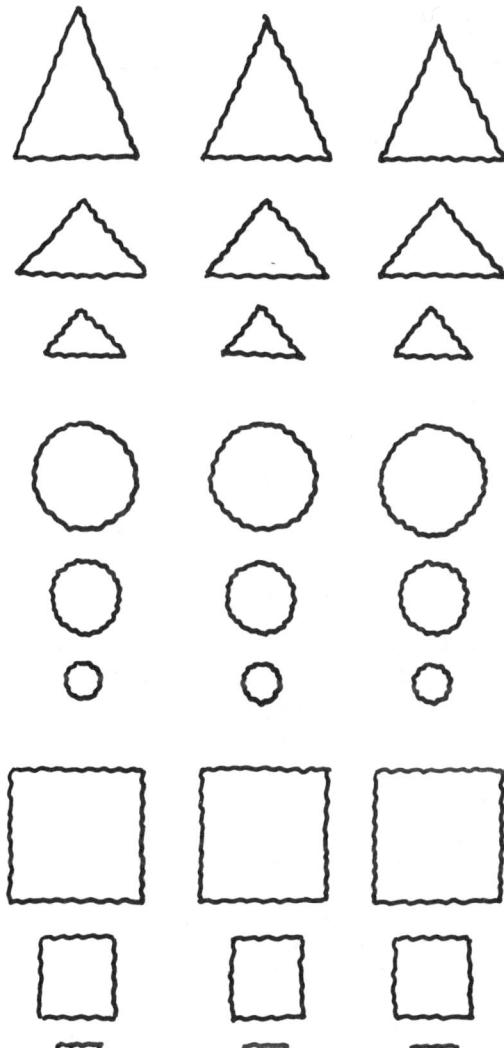

"Sorting Paper Shapes" can help children
- develop an awareness of similarities and differences.
- sort and classify according to likenesses and differences.

Give each child or each group of children a set of paper shapes in three colors, three shapes, and three sizes. To encourage sorting, ask the children to find the ones that are alike. Some of the children may separate the pieces by color (all reds, all blues, all yellows), others may separate them by size (big ones, little ones, middle-sized ones, etc.), and still others may sort them by shape (rectangle, triangle, circle, etc.). Help the children know that objects can be sorted in several different ways.

When everyone has finished, ask each child to tell you how the objects they sorted are alike and how they are different.

☞ **Note to the Teacher:** *You can keep the shapes for later use, such as for art projects, name tags, or other math activities.*

Materials

- *paper shapes in three colors, three shapes (circles, squares, triangles, etc.), and three sizes*

Shapes

Shape Designs

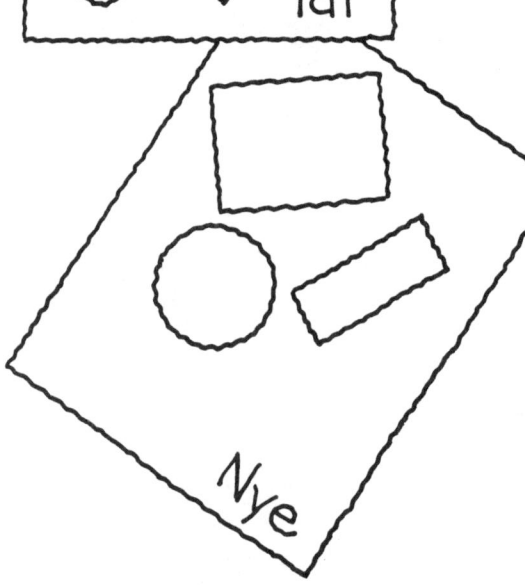

"Shape Designs" can help children
- develop an awareness of similarities and differences.
- understand and accept individual differences.

Show the children several different-colored, different-sized paper shapes. Talk about ways the paper shapes are alike and ways they are different, such as
- some are the same color, but have different shapes or sizes.
- some are the same shape, but are different in color or size.

Have the children point out as many differences as they can.

Give each child several shapes and a piece of construction paper. Invite the children to paste or glue their shapes onto their paper to make a collage. When the collages are done, point out that everyone's ideas are different, so each picture is different, too.

Materials

- different-colored, different-sized paper shapes (circles, squares, triangles, rectangles, long strips, etc.)
- paste or glue
- construction paper

Connect-the-Dot Designs

"Connect-the-Dot Designs" can help children
- learn more about shapes.
- develop their imagination.

In advance, make a "dot" design for each child by drawing lots of dots anywhere on each piece of paper, or have the children make their own dot designs.

Give each child a dot design, or use the one he or she made. The children can connect the dots with a pencil in any sequence to make a unique pattern or design. Have the children use crayons or markers to color their design however they wish.

Encourage each child to show his or her design to the class and talk about the shapes he or she sees in the design, such as triangles, squares, rectangles, or diamonds.

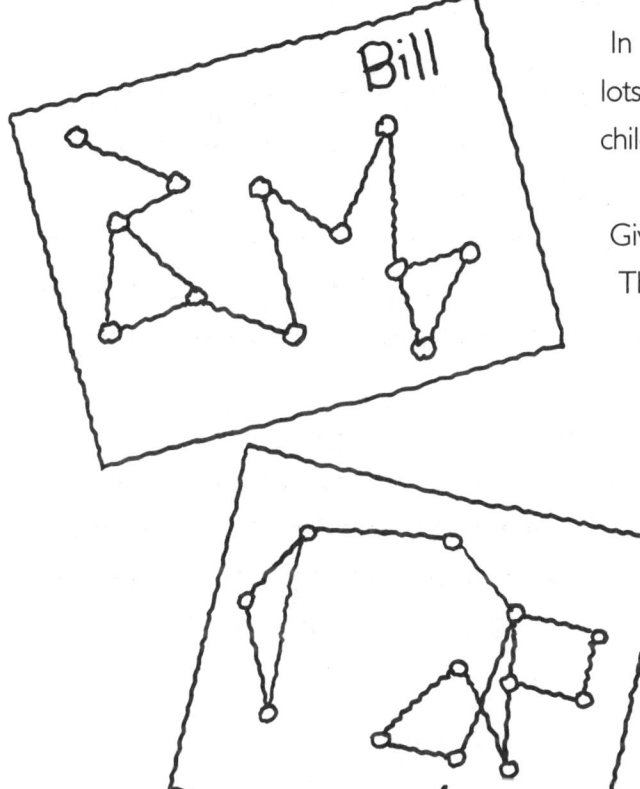

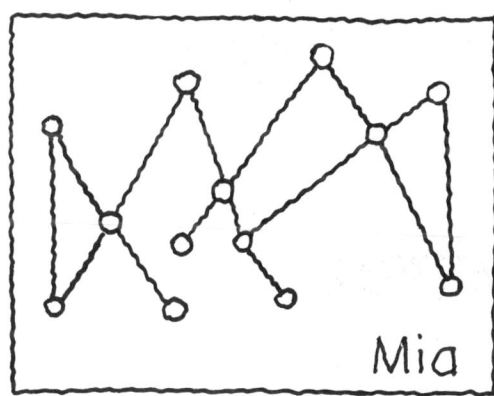

Materials
- paper
- pencils
- crayons or markers

Shapes

Puzzles

"Puzzles" can help children
- learn more about shapes.
- develop fine motor skills.

In advance, cut out several magazine pictures of cars, toys, or other objects. (The pictures will be used for puzzles, and some children might prefer not to cut up pictures of people or animals.)

Explain that puzzles show one large picture that has been divided into several different shapes. Then let each child make his or her own puzzle.

Give each child a magazine picture, and have him or her paste or glue it onto a piece of tagboard, being sure that all the edges are firmly attached.

After the paste or glue has dried, encourage each child to cut his or her picture into five or six pieces to make a puzzle. Show the children how to mix up their puzzle pieces and put them back together again. Children who want to can trade and play with classmates' puzzles as well.

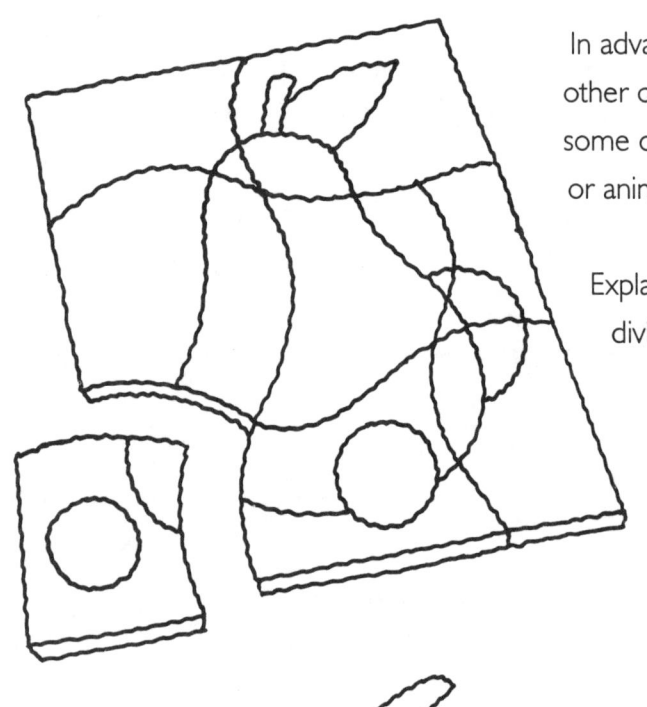

Materials
- magazine pictures of cars, toys, or other objects
- scissors
- paste or glue
- tagboard

Sizes & Measurements

Learning about size and measurement comes as children begin comparing objects. At first, they may sort things as "big" and "little." Later on, they may become ready to deal with a more sophisticated concept and *compare* shapes—"smaller than this one, but bigger than that one." That's what helps children understand about the relationship between one number and another. You can help children learn about size and measurement in everyday ways, such as through cooking activities, scientific exploration, and even physical education experiences. Through activities such as these, children understand why it helps to be able to measure length, width, weight, and time. Then these basic math concepts have meaning for them.

Literature Links

The Fattest, Tallest, Biggest Snowman Ever! by Marilyn Burns

I'm Growing by Aliki

Length (Math Counts) by Henry Pluckrose

Measure It! by Rozanne Lanczak Williams (Creative Teaching Press)

One Grain of Rice by Demi

Take Off with Time by Sally Hewitt

Ten Beads Tall illustrated by Pam Adams

Pouring Rice

"Pouring Rice" can help children
- learn more about their world.
- learn about conservation of volume.

Cover a work area with a tablecloth. Show several plastic containers of different sizes. Talk about each container, and ask the children to guess which containers will hold the most and the least.

Encourage the children to use measuring cups to fill the containers with rice, popcorn, dried beans, birdseed, or beads. Ask questions such as
- *Can you show me a cup that is full?*
- *If you poured rice from that container into this one, would this container be full, too?*

When the activity is over, let everyone empty the contents into a large storage container for use at another time.

Materials

- tablecloth
- plastic containers of different sizes
- measuring cups
- rice, popcorn, dried beans, birdseed, or beads
- large storage container

Making a Graph

"Making a Graph" can help children
- develop an awareness of similarities and differences.
- sort and classify according to likenesses and differences.
- develop an understanding of the concept of size.

Ask the children to talk about their favorite colors, and show them a way to graph the information. To do this, make a chart on butcher paper with the names of several colors across the bottom. (Use a coordinating colored marker to write each name.) Then give each child an index card with his or her name on it. Have children take turns attaching their card above the name of their favorite color to make a simple bar graph.

Have the children count how many cards are in each column, and write the numbers under the color names.

Our Favorite Colors

red	black	yellow	green	orange	blue
	Fay				
Ty	Gary			Dan	
Chen	Pam	Lu		Lon	Bill
J.J.	Vic	Jo	Sam	Po	Tam

Materials
- butcher paper
- markers
- index cards

Sizes & Measurements

Comparing Sizes

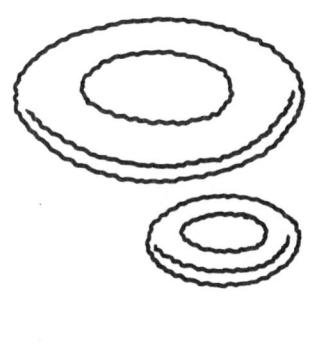

"Comparing Sizes" can help children
- develop an awareness of similarities and differences.
- learn more about their world.

To help the children become familiar with the concept of size, play some comparison games with them. Start with something simple, such as comparing your shoe to a child's shoe. Ask the children to tell you which one is bigger and which is smaller. Then have the children compare other things, such as a

- teaspoon and soupspoon.
- dinner plate and saucer.
- cereal box and pudding box.
- large bowl and small bowl.
- toy car and an actual automobile.
- grown-up's coat and a child's coat.

Then choose an item from the classroom, such as a pencil. Ask the children to find something bigger than the pencil. Show another item, and have the children find something smaller. As you show other items, ask the children if the things they find are a lot bigger or smaller than what you just named or just a little bigger or smaller.

For a third game, arrange four or five objects from biggest to smallest. Move them around while the children turn their backs, and then see if they can put the objects back in order. Play several rounds of the game with different items.

Materials
- *household items (silverware, dishes, empty food boxes, dollhouse furniture, toys, etc.)*
- *classroom items (pencils, books, desks, chairs, etc.)*

Sizes & Measurements

# How Long?

"How Long?" can help children
- learn more about their world.
- develop healthy curiosity.
- make comparisons.

Talk about what people use to measure how long things are, such as a ruler. Then tell children that you can use almost anything to measure, such as your hands, your feet, a piece of string, or a block. Give each child a piece of string and a block, and encourage the children to use them and their hands and feet to measure objects around the room. As the children measure, ask questions such as

- *How many hands long is the table?*
- *Using string, how tall are you?*
- *How many "feet" long is it from the door to your desk if you walked heel to toe?*

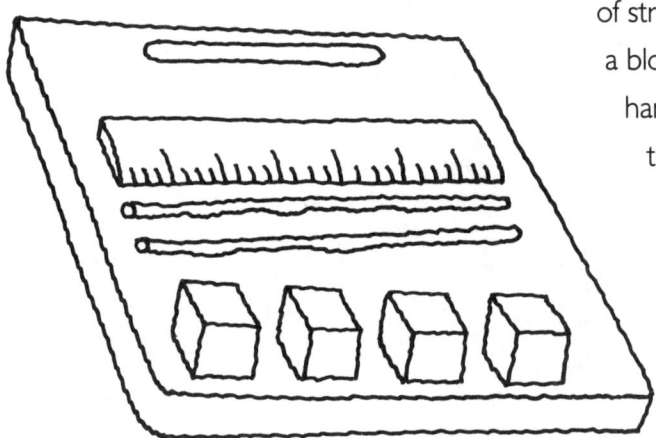

After the activity, you might want to encourage dramatic play about measuring. If you set out a box with paper, pencils, tape measures, and rulers, along with a carpenter's hat or a tool box with plastic tools, the children can pretend to build something, such as a community center or a playground. You could encourage the children to measure things as they pretend to build.

Materials

- 12" (30.5 cm) pieces of string
- blocks
- box with paper, pencils, tape measures, and rulers (optional)
- carpenter's hat or a tool box with plastic tools (optional)

Sizes & Measurements

Comparing Weights

"Comparing Weights" can help children
- learn more about their world.
- develop healthy curiosity.
- make comparisons.

Make a simple balance scale. Use a hole punch to make four holes around the top of two paper cups. Tie a string through each hole. For each cup, gather and tie all four strings around the end of a ruler or yardstick so there is a hanging cup at each end. Balance the ruler or yardstick on three of your fingers or your hand.

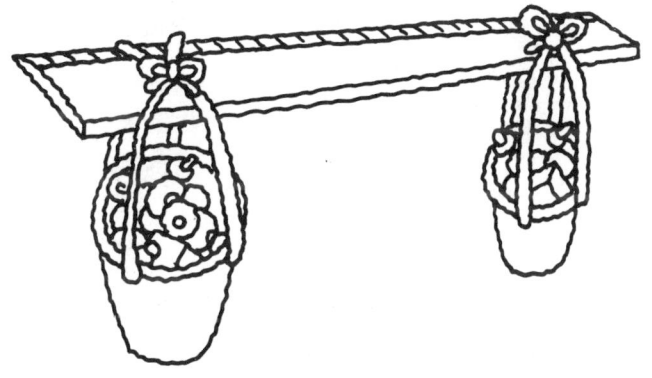

Display a variety of small objects. Invite a child to choose an object and place it in one of the cups. Ask the children to talk about what happens. Next, have a child place one object in one cup and a different object in the other cup. Have the children talk about which object is heavier and why they think so. If the objects balance, point out that the objects probably have the same weight. Encourage the children to experiment with all of the objects before placing the scale and the objects in a learning center.

The children might enjoy pretending to be scales. With their arms stretched out at their sides, they can bend from side to side, tipping like scales, at your suggestions. For example, you might say *What would happen if there were a bowling ball in your left hand and a feather in your right hand?*

Materials
- hole punch
- two paper cups
- eight 12" (30.5 cm) pieces of heavy string
- ruler or yardstick
- objects that will fit in the cups (beans, rubber bands, coins, toy cars or toy people, blocks, clay, etc.)

Measuring Time

"Measuring Time" can help children
- learn more about time.
- develop an awareness of similarities and differences.

Ask the children to talk about ways people measure time. Show the children a variety of objects used to measure time, and talk about each one. Explain that these things help grown-ups know what time it is or how much time has passed. Then encourage the children to look through old magazines or catalogs to find objects that measure time.

After the children have had some time to look for objects, ask them to tell you how they know what time it is. To help the children with ideas, ask questions such as
- How do you know when it's time to get up?
- How do you know when to get ready for lunch?
- How do you know it's recess time?
- How do you know when school is over?

☞ **Note to the Teacher:** It's a good idea to display a schedule showing what the children do during the day. Older children might want to know that naptime is one hour long or that story time lasts about ten minutes. This will help them begin to understand about measuring time.

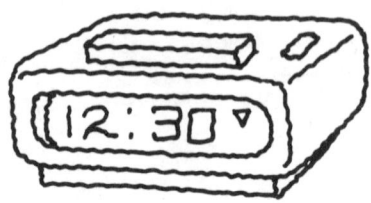

Materials
- objects that measure time (alarm clock, watch, stopwatch, hourglass, egg timer, etc.)
- old magazines or catalogs

Sizes & Measurements

Sand Clock

"Sand Clock" can help children
- learn more about time.
- develop an awareness of similarities and differences.

To begin, take the children on a tour of the school to look for clocks. Explain that clocks are a way for people to measure time and find out how much time has passed since something began or how much time they have to wait before something begins.

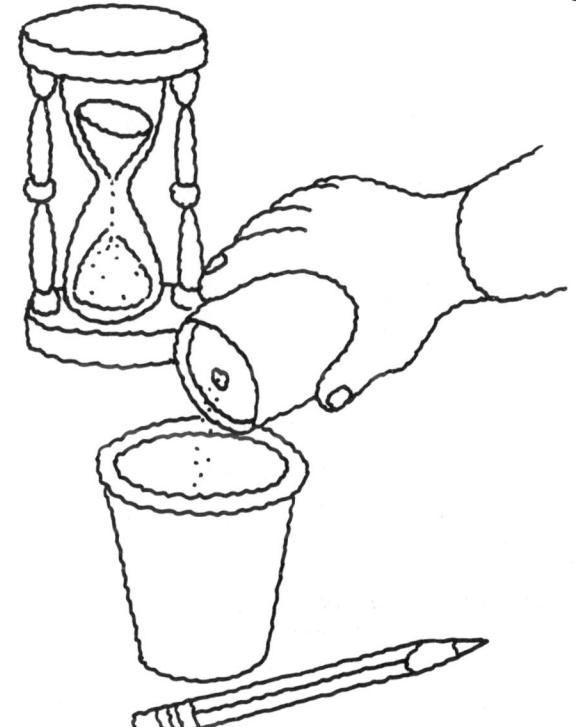

Back in class, show the children how to make a sand clock that measures time. Fill a paper cup with sand. Use a sharp pencil to poke a hole in the bottom of a second cup. Cover the hole with your finger and pour the sand into the cup with the hole. Move your finger and show the children how the sand runs through the hole into the other cup.

Explain that people can measure time by counting how long it takes for all the sand to run out. Sift the sand through the second cup again, and have the children count with you until all the sand is in the first cup.

Then use the sand clock to measure how long it takes children to do something, such as
- say the alphabet.
- jump in place 20 times.
- shake hands with five people.

Materials
- two paper cups
- sand
- sharp pencil

Sizes & Measurements

Mister Rogers' Neighborhood Television Program References

Mister Rogers' Neighborhood is the longest-running series on PBS. Every program addresses themes that are important in the lives of children and families.

Learning about numbers, shapes, and sizes is an everyday feature of the Neighborhood series. The programs listed here are more directly related to the particular activities in this book. You may want to watch these programs with the children to help them appreciate and value the concepts of number, shape, and size. After viewing a program, you might want to present an activity from this book.

Feel free to call your local PBS station for the broadcast schedule. You can also receive an annual schedule by sending a self-addressed, stamped envelope to Family Communications, 4802 Fifth Avenue, Pittsburgh, PA 15213, or by checking their Web site at *www.misterrogers.org*.

Schools can make a videotaped copy of a *Mister Rogers' Neighborhood* program and hold it for use in that school for one year. Child care providers can tape a program and hold it for use in that child care setting for seven years.

Numbers
Looking for Numbers: Programs 1633 and 1698
How Many Times?: Program 1518
Ball Bounce: Programs 1602 and 1604
Boxes inside Boxes: Program 1589

Shapes
Wheel Toys: Programs 1567, 1631, 1682, and 1699
Blocks: Programs 1500 and 1606
My Shape It Has Three Corners: Program 1674
Three-Cornered Hats: Program 1675
Puzzles: Programs 1618 and 1718

Sizes & Measurements
Making a Graph: Program 1651
Comparing Sizes: Programs 1732 and 1735

Related Theme Weeks
GAMES: Programs 1511–1515
FOOD: Programs 1536–1540
MUSIC: Programs 1546–1550
ALIKE & DIFFERENT: Programs 1581–1585
"JOSEPHINE THE SHORT-NECK GIRAFFE": Programs 1606–1610
THINGS TO WEAR: Programs 1671–1675
FAST & SLOW: Programs 1681–1684
BIG & LITTLE: Programs 1731–1735